SERBIA TO KUT.

SERBIA TO KÛT

AN ACCOUNT OF

THE WAR IN THE BIBLE LANDS.

BY

JOSEPH T. PARFIT, M.A.

Canon of St. George's, Jerusalem.

(Author of "Twenty Years in Baghdad and Syria.")

ILLUSTRATED.

The Naval & Military Press Ltd

Published by
The Naval & Military Press Ltd
5 Riverside, Brambleside, Bellbrook
Industrial Estate, Uckfield, East Sussex,
TN22 1QQ England

Tel: +44 (0) 1825 749494
Fax: +44 (0) 1825 765701

www.naval-military-press.com
www.military-genealogy.com

CONTENTS.

LIST OF ILLUSTRATIONS.

NOTE.

The **numbers** printed in brackets refer to a set of 68 lantern
slides which have been prepared to illustrate the subject-matter when
read as a lantern lecture. The complete set of slides and copies of
this book can be obtained from Messrs. Newton & Co., King Street,
Covent Garden. The italic **letters** in brackets refer to notes on
Bible places, which will be found at the end of each section.

PREFATORY NOTE.

The author of the following brief chapters has attempted to bring together in an attractive form, the salient features of the great war as it has been waged throughout the ancient lands of the Bible. He is indebted to various authorities in the compilation of this record, and desires especially to acknowledge his obligation to "*The Times*" newspaper and its invaluable "History of the War." Though originally written as a lantern lecture, the book is now published in its present form because the subject-matter and the illustrations are likely to prove of permanent interest to the general reader.

Sketch map of "Germany's Corridor from the North Sea to the Persian Gulf."

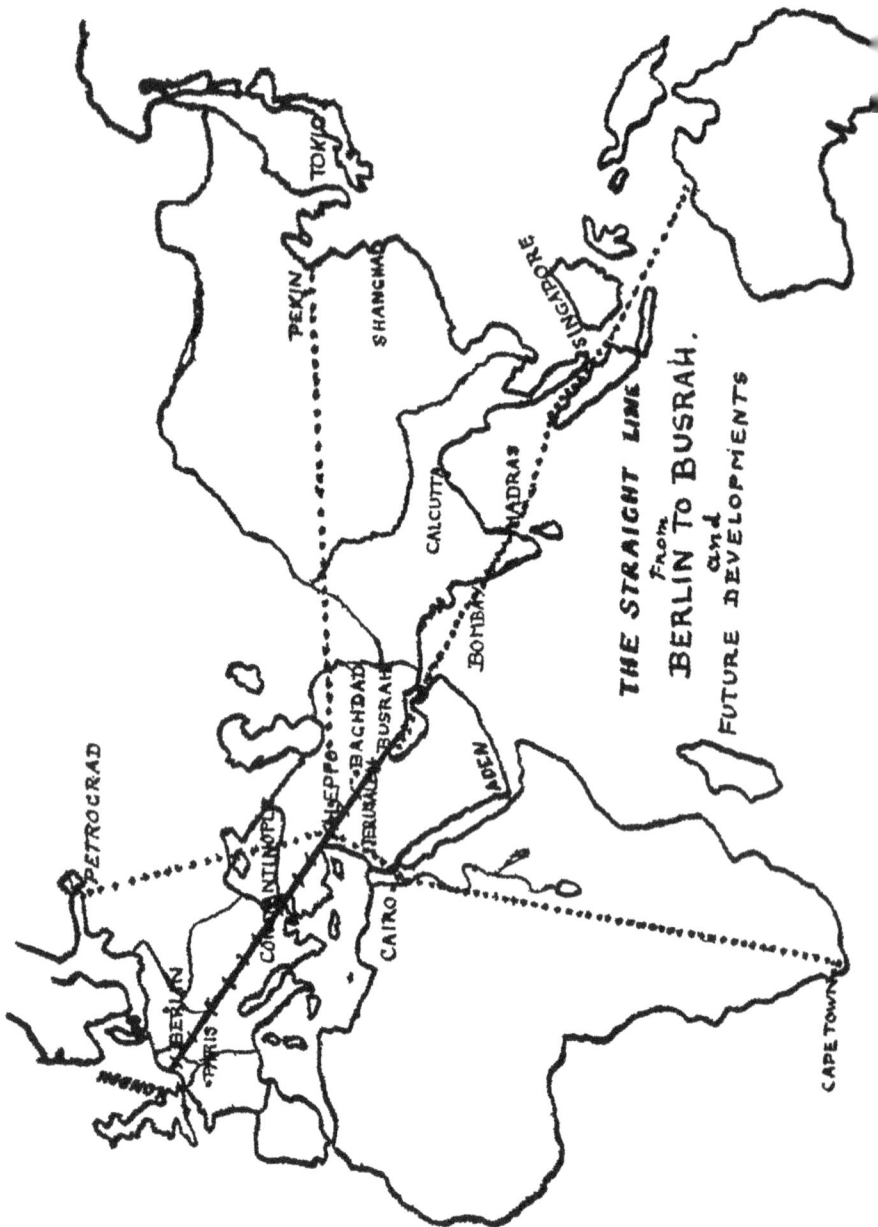

SERBIA TO KÛT.

I.

The Geography of the War in the Near East.

(*1*) The Lands of the Bible occupy a central position in the Eastern Hemisphere uniting the three continents of Europe, Asia and Africa, and Germany's schemes for world dominion have brought these ancient lands into the very vortex of the great whirlpool of war. The proposed German corridor through the Balkan States and Mesopotamia is practically a straight line from the North Sea to the Persian Gulf, the possession of which would have placed the shortest route to India and the East entirely under German control. *The Times* told us on August 3rd, 1914, that "the war began with Serbia *(a)* because Serbia was the chief obstacle

to the Austro-German advance towards the
Mediterranean at Salonica, and to the establishment of complete German control of the
Balkans, the Dardanelles, Asia Minor, and the
land and sea routes to Egypt and India."

For the accomplishment of these schemes
it was necessary to secure Turkey as Germany's
ally, so the Kaiser paid a pilgrimage to Jerusalem in 1898, when he ratified the compact
with the Sultan which gave him permission to
construct the Baghdad Railway from Constantinople to the Persian Gulf, and in return for
these privileges he ventured to promise Turkey
a magnificent reward.   (2) It was then he persuaded the Sultan to initiate a Pan-Islamic
Crusade which would prepare the whole of the
Mohammedan world for the great day when
Germany would restore Egypt to the Ottoman
Empire and make Cairo the capital of a
Pan-Islamic kingdom that would embrace the
whole of the Mohammedan lands from Morocco
to Calcutta.   This was the Kaiser's dream which
captivated Enver Pasha and the Young Turks
when they inherited from Abdul Hamid the
ruined remnants of the Ottoman Empire.   It is
very important to keep in mind a general
impression of the geographical situation in order

to follow intelligently the developments of the
war in the Bible Lands.

(a) **Serbia,** where the great War began, was visited by St. Paul
when he passed through Apollonia and Amphipolis (Acts xvii. 1), and
"fully preached the Gospel with mighty signs and wonders unto
Illyricum" (Rom. xv. 19). This included Dalmatia (2 Tim. iv. 10),
and the two names were used for the same extensive region along the
Adriatic Sea. On his second missionary journey the great apostle
must have traversed a considerable portion of the Balkan States. When
the vision called him to Macedonia, he passed by Mudros and the
peninsula of Gallipoli. He proceeded to Neapolis and Philippi, not far
from the modern Kavalla, where the earthquake burst open his prison
doors and led to the jailor's conversion (Acts xvi. 11).

II.

Why Turkey tottered and Busrah fell.

(3) Every pilgrimage to the Holy Land naturally begins at Jaffa, (b) and right well will the traveller to Jerusalem remember the awful difficulty of passing in a small boat through the dangerous rocks that bar the approach to the landing stage. It was quite impossible in stormy weather for passengers to disembark here at all, and although an immense amount of wealth has been brought annually to Palestine by thousands of tourists, yet the neglected condition of this important port illustrates the ineptitude of the Turks to govern or improve any country that had the misfortune to fall into their hands. The striking contrast between Egypt and Palestine caused the majority of the inhabitants of the Holy Land to hope for the expulsion of the Turk, and the advent of a British Protectorate.

(4) Here, in the Biblical Joppa, not far from the traditional house of Simon the Tanner, an enormous gathering of Moslems was convened

4

Map of the Mohammedan world.

House of Simon the Tanner in Jaffa. (*page 4*).

Water pipes stored in Alexandretta for use in attack on Suez Canal.
(*page 10*).

soon after the declaration of war against England.

(5) The people were assembled in the market place, around the Government House, over which the Turkish flag was flying from a massive flag-staff. They were listening to speeches that were being delivered by the Turkish officials and the religious chiefs. " Be loyal," cried the orators, "to your Sultan, to your country, to your religion, and to Germany, our faithful ally, that has now adopted our Moslem Faith, that has risen to rescue it from the infidel English, who are trying to wipe out the religion of Islam. If you will read the German papers you will see what atrocities England is perpetrating in Egypt and India upon our Moslem brethren. There, our Holy Days are despised, and our mosques are being torn down—to the " Jehad " then, to the Holy War by order of our Sultan—let us wipe out the infidel English, the French and the Russians —let us break their power." And just then something *did* break, for with a great crash the massive flag-staff snapped in two, and the Turkish standard came hurtling down into the midst of the horrified crowd. The superstitious people were alarmed at this evil omen, the

Moslem priests tried to reassure them, but the
crowd gradually dispersed while the orators
were breathing curses on the infidels and
threatening some day to cut their throats
This incident was related that night to an
Englishman who was then interned at Jaffa,
and he laughingly exclaimed to his informant,
" the old flag-staff must have been rotten for
years." " Yes," said the friend who related the
incident, " that's it exactly, it is a correct omen ;
the Turkish Government has been rotten for
years, and we feel certain it is now about to fall."
(6) On the very same day the news reached
England from the Persian Gulf that British
forces had taken possession of the important
Turkish town of Busrah, the chief port of
Mesopotamia. (c)

Busrah is situated on the right bank of
the great Shat 'l Arab, nearly 70 miles up the
river from the head of the Persian Gulf, and it
was intended to be the temporary terminus of
the German Baghdad Railway. Six weeks
before the outbreak of war, a British intelligence
officer sent to Busrah a young Afghan, who, on
arrival, said to the Turkish officials, " I hear
there is going to be a Holy War." They
welcomed him with open arms, as they hoped

some day to stir up the inhabitants of Afghanistan, so they gave him freedom to go about, and he watched the German officers instruct the Turkish gunners as to where they should hide their guns and conceal their batteries amongst the date palms that line the banks of the Shat 'l Arab. Two weeks before the outbreak of war, this young Afghan slipped out of the country and found his chief with a force of 5,000 British-Indian troops under the command of General Delamain, (7) already in transports half-way up the Persian Gulf at Bahrain. (d) He presented his report, and, a few days later, as soon as war was declared, British warships escorted the transports to the Shat 'l Arab, when, to the astonishment of the Germans, they were able rapidly to locate and destroy the concealed Turkish batteries, for the simple reason that the British secret service is far more secret and much more efficient than that of the Germans.

(b) **Jaffa**=Joppa. Hiram, king of Tyre, sent wood from the Lebanon to Joppa for Solomon's temple (2 Chron. ii. 16). Jonah went to Joppa when he fled to Tarshish (Jonah i. 3). St. Peter healed Tabitha at Joppa (Acts ix. 36) and stayed in the house of Simon the Tanner (Acts ix. 43). Here also he saw the vision which led to the reception of Cornelius, the Gentile proselyte, into the Christian Church (Acts x.).

(c) **Mesopotamia** is frequently mentioned in the earlier books of the Bible. Nahor, Bethuel, and Laban dwelt at Ur of the Chaldees

(Gen xxiv. 10), near the town of Nasiriyeh, which is now a British military base on the Euphrates.   Abraham was born here, also Rebekah, the wife of Isaac, and Rachael and Leah, the wives of Jacob, who dwelt 21 years in Mesopotamia.   Balaam came from this region (Deut. xxiii. 4), and the children of Ammon hired chariots and horsemen out of Mesopotamia when they fought against King David (1 Chron. xix. 6).   This is the country of the great Babylonian and Assyrian monarchies.

(*d*) **Bahrain** : The islands of Bahrain contain about 12 square miles of Phœnician mounds, and a description of the Phœnician temples that once existed here is to be found in the writings of Strabo. Many writers identify Bahrain with **Dedan,** mentioned in Ezekiel xxvii. 15.

III.

German Railways and Water Pipes.

(8) Before we proceed to follow the fortunes of the Mesopotamian Expedition it is necessary to refer to the German scheme for the Baghdad railway. The concessions for this railway were obtained by the Kaiser nearly twenty years ago, and rapid strides have been made with its construction, for Germany hoped that within a few years the completed line would be linked up with the existing railway system from Berlin to Constantinople. The Persian Gulf terminus of the railway was originally intended to be at Koweit, but England successfully resisted the efforts made by Germany to establish a naval base at the head of the Persian Gulf, so after many years' negotiation, Germany agreed to terminate the railway temporarily at Busrah. In return for this concession to us, we yielded permission to Germany to make a branch line of the Baghdad railway to the Syrian port of (9) Alexandretta, *(e)* with permission also to construct a railway jetty there for commercial purposes.

Some months afterwards one of our engineers reported that the designs for this railway jetty had expanded into plans for a harbour big enough to contain the German fleet, and strong defensive positions were being rapidly constructed by the Germans at this strategic Mediterranean port.

(*10*) It was here at Alexandretta, nearly three years before the outbreak of war, that a photograph was taken which subsequently proved to be peculiarly interesting. It was a snapshot of one of the many piles of water pipes that Germany accumulated at this port. Nobody then knew what they were for, but we now know that they were intended for the long projected expedition against Egypt. Since the war began, the Germans have hurriedly completed a new railway right through Palestine down to Beersheba (*f*) and across the Egyptian frontier. These water pipes have been conveyed to the south of Palestine from Alexandretta, and have been laid across the dry desert for many miles (*g*) in order to supply water to the German and Turkish troops in their advance towards the Suez Canal. (*h*) We were surprised to read one day in our newspapers that even in the rainless month of May,

1916, 4,000 Turkish troops were able to come within 15 miles of the Suez Canal, and 1,000 German soldiers attacked our outposts within 30 miles of Port Said. This could only have been possible by the aid of the water supply conveyed through these miles of pipes which had been prepared for this very purpose in Alexandretta three years before war began.

(*11*) Beyrout (*i*) is another place where similar preparations were in progress before the declaration of war. In March, 1914, great quantities of rails were landed there, intended professedly for the Baghdad Railway, but in reality for the new line to Beersheba and Egypt. Five hundred tons of dynamite also were brought in by a German ship, for conveyance with the Turkish troops to the Suez Canal, as a German General declared, "for breaking the spine of the British Empire."

(*e*) **Alexandretta** is a seaport situated not far from the Biblical town of Antioch, where the followers of Jesus were first called Christians (Acts xi. 27, and Acts xv. 30).

(*f*) **Beersheba** was the home of Abraham after the birth of Isaac (Gen. xxii. 19), and it was here that God appeared to Jacob on his way to Egypt (Gen. xxviii. 10). Elijah also came to Beersheba when he fled from the wicked Jezebel (1 Kings xix. 3). It was the headquarters of the American Red Cross contingent, under Dr. St. John Ward, during the first Turkish attack on the Suez Canal.

(*g*) The desert that lies around Beersheba and extends towards the Suez Canal was known to Abraham as the **Wilderness of Shur**, to

which Hagar fled with her son Ishmael (Gen. xxi., 14) whose
descendants subsequently inhabited this region (Gen. xxv. 18), and in
the time of Saul some portion of the country was peopled by the
Amalekites (1 Sam. xv. 7).

(*h*) The **Suez Canal** runs through the borders of the Biblical Land
of Goshen.   The main body of the Turks in their attack on the Canal
followed the caravan route which was taken by Joseph, and subsequently by his brethren, when they went down into Egypt; the same
road, doubtless, that was traversed by Joseph and Mary when they fled
to Egypt with the Infant Christ (Gen. xlv. 10 ; Matt. ii. 14).   Moses
led the children of Israel out of the land of Goshen at a point not far
from Suez, and thence along the shores of the Sinaitic peninsula to the
Mount where the Ten Commandments were given, and from there to
what is now the port of Akabah.

(*i*) **Beyrout** is the chief port of Syria at the foot of Mount
Lebanon, situated in a beautiful bay a few miles north of Tyre and
Sidon.   A French railway connects Beyrout with Damascus.

IV.

The Spine of the British Empire.

(*12*) It was of the utmost importance to the British Empire that the Suez Canal should be adequately guarded. To keep open this vital artery of our communications was a prime necessity to us, consequently many thousands of troops were drafted into Egypt with all possible speed. The Turks fully anticipated that as soon as their troops appeared within reach of the Suez Canal, the Egyptian Mohammedans would revolt against the British Government. There was one man especially who understood the seriousness of the situation in Egypt. He knew the Near East remarkably well, he had learned Arabic in Palestine, he had surveyed the hills and valleys of the Holy Land, and had helped to produce a beautiful map of Western Palestine, published by the Palestine Exploration Fund. He afterwards became famous for his remarkable conquest of the Soudan and its subsequent pacification. He made a deep impression upon the peasantry of Egypt by the care he took to guard their interests when he introduced the Five Feddans Law, which protected their humble homesteads from voracious money-lenders. This tireless organiser who won the hearts of the Egyptians, whose foresight and heroism did so much to guard the vital interests of the British Empire, was none other than Lord Kitchener. (*13*) It will be remembered that he was on his way to Egypt when he was called back from France to take charge of the War Office in London. The following poem appeared in *The Times* on Tuesday, June 13th, 1916, after his tragic death at sea off the coast of Scotland.

LORD KITCHENER.

Unflinching hero, watchful to foresee
And face thy country's peril wheresoe'er,
Directing war and peace with equal care,
Till by long toil ennobled thou wert he
Whom England called and bade " Set my arm free
To obey my will and save my honour fair "—
What day the foe presumed on her despair
And she herself had trust in none but thee :
Among Herculean deeds the miracle
That mass'd the labour of ten years in one
Shall be thy monument.   Thy work is done
Ere we could thank thee ; and the high sea swell
Surgeth unheeding where thy proud ship fell
By the lone Orkneys, ere the set of sun.

June 8th.   ROBERT BRIDGES.

(*14*) Thanks to Lord Kitchener the first expedition organised by the Turks against the Suez Canal proved a dismal failure. The whole long line of the Canal was by that time admirably guarded, and the Turkish attack, though courageously carried out after a difficult journey across a waterless desert, was effectively repulsed, and numbers of Turkish soldiers were taken captive by our troops. The Turks carried some of their drinking water in a number of collapsible boats which were utilised, when the canal was reached, in the attempt to effect a crossing.

Every Turkish soldier as he passed through Palestine was provided with two sacks and an empty petroleum tin. On reaching the Canal he was expected to fill the sacks with sand, throw them into the Canal, and thus, besides blocking the Canal, he would help to form a bridge across to the other side. If this failed the petroleum tin would be used to buoy him up while he paddled across into Egypt. One of the first prisoners taken at the Canal said he was a coachman from Jerusalem. The Turks had pulled him off the box of his carriage and said, "Now you are a soldier." Then they hounded him across the desert to fight against

the English, and like many others he was
thankful to be taken prisoner.

(*15*) The Turkish Government had made a
desperate effort to enlist the sympathy and
support of certain Bedouin tribes. These were
led to believe that the Germans had all become
Mohammedans, that the Holy War was spread-
ing in Egypt and in India, and that the whole
of the Egyptians would welcome them with
open arms.

While the Turks were making their march
across the Biblical desert of Shur, some of the
more ignorant Egyptians were filled with great
hopes and expectations. The millennium was
coming—the golden age. They were confident
that the Turk would very easily get into the
country. When asked how they would manage
it these Egyptians replied :—" Oh, the Turks
have 60,000 camels, which will be very valuable
for transporting men across the desert; but in
the last six days the camels will not be given
any water to drink, and then, when they get to
the Canal's edge, 60,000 camels will rush
forward and drink the Canal dry." They forgot
that the water flowed in from the deep salt sea
at both ends of the Canal. Some said, that the

Turkish prisoners of war under Indian guard at Suez Canal.
(*page 15*).

The Beilan Pass, near Alexandretta. (*page 23.*)

The Citadel at Aleppo, headquarters of the German railways.
(*page 23*).

backs of the camels were to be covered with pitch and set alight, the camels would jump into the Canal and form a bridge, across which the Turks would pass. When these Egyptians realised that the Turks had been beaten off, by one of those strange turns of thought and feeling they said:—" The Turk! What has he ever done for us? Dog! Let him die in the desert!" Some of the more degraded robber tribes from the East of the Jordan were persuaded to join the Turkish expedition, and a (16) few of these were amongst the prisoners captured in a miserable condition as they reached the Canal. Those of the Bedouin who escaped capture, retired in disgust, and carried away the horses and the arms that had been supplied to them by the Turks. These irregular forces, recruited from the Bedouin, began to understand that they had been deceived, so they returned once more to their encampments in the desert, and no doubt subsequently joined the revolt of the more stedfast Arabs in Arabia. (j)

(j) **Arabia.** When St. Paul went from Damascus into Arabia he probably travelled eastward towards Mesopotamia, or else towards the south by the regular caravan route into the heart of Arabia. Arabians were present in Jerusalem on the day of Pentecost (Acts ii. 11).

V.

Turkey's Capital, Roadsteads and Ports.

(*17*) If the Gallipoli expedition (Note *a*), was in some ways a lamentable failure, it nevertheless kept the Turkish forces busily occupied whilst our Suez Canal defences were being rapidly strengthened. The *New Statesman* in an article published on June 10th, 1916, declared that Lord Kitchener was opposed to the Dardanelles expedition, and that his alternative policy was the sending of an expedition on a large scale to Alexandretta. Had this been undertaken, we can perhaps conclude, in the light of what the Russian accomplished at Erzeroum, Bitlis, and Trebizond that it would possibly have proved a more effective way of dealing with the Turk and perhaps hastened the opening of the Dardanelles.

(*18*) Russia has long desired a free outlet for her commerce through the Bosphorus to the Mediterranean, and Viscount Grey has publicly stated that this must certainly be conceded to

her at the conclusion of the war. The
Bosphorus is one of the most beautiful places in
the world. It is intended that the Russian
advance through Armenia should eventually
terminate with the occupation of its southern
shores, and it seems probable that this struggle
will continue until the Allied forces in some way
or other succeed in reaching the city of
Constantinople.

In January, 1916, the Germans sent
80,000 German soldiers into the city, and it was
said that they had established guns in such
positions as to ensure the destruction of the
Ottoman capital if ever they were compelled to
evacuate it. The whole civilized world con-
template with some amount of anxiety the
possible fate of the famous Church of St.
Sophia, (19) which was built as a Christian
Cathedral, and has been in the hands of the
Mohammedans for nearly 500 years, The
Russian peasantry and the whole of the Eastern
Christians are particularly keen upon the
restoration of this beautiful Cathedral to
Christian worship.

After the evacuation of Gallipoli the Allied
Navies maintained a strict blockade of the coast

of Asia Minor, Syria, and Palestine. Frequent attacks were made by monitors and aeroplanes upon the fortified positions around the Gulf of (20) Smyrna. (k)

This was one of the ports in Turkey where British trade flourished, so that with the out-break of war numbers of the foreign residents were interned here, or were carried off to the internment camps in the interior. The im-portant port of Alexandretta was also frequently visited by British and French warships. In January, 1915, a British warship destroyed the railway bridges, the station and other strategic positions connected with the German Baghdad Railway. Whilst this was being done, Djemal Pasha was mobilising large forces of Turkish troops in the city of (21) Damascus. (l)

He suddenly ordered about 90 Englishmen and Frenchmen to be shut up in a dirty, vermin-stricken native hotel. They were kept there for three days and three nights under most trying circumstances, and Djemal Pasha threatened to shoot every one of them unless our Commander stopped, as he said, "bom-barding the undefended port of Alexandretta." A telegram was therefore sent to Alexandretta, and when it was received our Commander called

up the governor of the city, told him he was
insulted, for the governor knew well that the
town of Alexandretta (22) had not been touched,
but that only the strategic works belonging to
the railway had been destroyed.

The governor was compelled to send a
telegram back to Djemal Pasha giving details
of what had happened, and telling him that he
would be held personally responsible for the
safety of the Englishmen. The Commander
added that he would now destroy two new
German locomotives as a further punishment
for Djemal Pasha's action. The Turkish
governor tremblingly asked our Commander to
fire no more shots, as the people were excited,
and he himself promised to blow up the locomotives if our Commander insisted upon their
destruction. The next day he came to apologise,
as he was unable to find anyone on shore
courageous enough to handle the explosives.
"Would the Commander," he said, "kindly
send off some of his men to do this dangerous
work if he still insisted upon their destruction,
but would he also allow them to wear the
Turkish Fez so that the people might think
they belonged to the Turkish army?" The
Commander consented on condition that our

blue-jackets were saluted by the Turkish troops as superior officers. So, on the following day, our men had an interesting experience when they strutted before the Turkish troops with Turkish fezes on their heads, and went off to destroy the German locomotives.

(*k*) **Smyrna** has retained its Biblical name. Its church was one of the seven churches in Asia Minor to which special exhortations were addressed by St. John in the Apocalypse (Rev. ii. 8).

(*l*) **Damascus** is one of the oldest and most beautifully situated cities of the world. Abraham's faithful steward Eliezer was a native of Damascus (Gen. xv. 2), and here the patriarch stayed for some time on his way from Mesopotamia to Palestine. The kings of Israel and Judah were constantly at war with the kings of Damascus, notably Benhadad (1 Kings xx. 1) and Hazael (2 Kings viii. 28). It was in Damascus that St. Paul met with Ananias and received his commission as the apostle to the Gentiles (Acts ix. 17).

VI.

From Alexandretta to Nineveh.

(*23*) There may be important reasons why the Allies have not landed troops at Alexandretta, though it is so near the junction of the great Baghdad Railway and the line that leads through Palestine to Egypt. It is supposed that the Beilan Pass is one real difficulty, for Alexandretta is backed by a mountain range that has been well fortified, and this is the only road that winds through the mountains and thence across the plains to Aleppo. (*24*) Important military depôts, ammunition stores, and enormous camps for German and Turkish troops have been established on the hill tops north of Alexandretta.

The headquarters of the German railway enterprises in Asiatic Turkey are established in Aleppo. (*25*) Four hundred German officials were residing here, all connected with the railway, just before the outbreak of war, and many thousands of German troops have passed through Aleppo on their way to Baghdad or

Palestine since the war began. The great railway station has been built upon a scale that foreshadows through communication from Berlin to Busrah. The tunnels through the Taurus and Amanus ranges have not yet been completed, neither has the magnificent bridge that is to span the Euphrates near the ancient city of Carchemish *(m)* where British archæologists have been excavating the mound at Jerabalus, which covers the ruins of the ancient Hittite capital.

Good roads however have been made in order to facilitate military transport, where the (26) permanent lines are still incomplete ; a temporary bridge has long ago been erected across the Tigris, and the railway has been rapidly extended towards Mosul (Nineveh) since the outbreak of the war. It is now possible for German officers to get from Berlin to Beersheba, near the Egyptian frontier, in six or seven days, and from Berlin to Baghdad in eight or nine days.

British civilian prisoners from Palestine and (27) Syria were brought through Aleppo and many of them, including the women and children, were marched to and fro across the bridge at

Temporary bridge of the German Baghdad railway across the Euphrates. (*page 24*).

Two views of bridge across the Tigris at Mosul (Nineveh). (*page 25*).

Jerabalus six or seven times whilst a German officer was taking moving photographs, for reproduction in the cinemas of Germany of these so-called " crowds of British prisoners crossing the Euphrates." Most of the British residents from Syria were interned at a place called (28) Urfa, where they were residing in a monastery at the time when the Armenian massacres began. They were subsequently transferred to Nigdi, not far from the ancient Cæsarea in Cappadocia. (*n*) The British residents from Baghdad were interned for a time in Mosul, which is the modern city on the right bank of the Tigris, opposite the ruins of ancient (29) Nineveh. (*o*) Near the right bank is a pontoon bridge that moves with the rise and fall of the river. This is joined to a long stone bridge that stretches across that portion of the river bed, which is only flooded when the river rises in the spring with the melting of the snows on the mountains. The road from the bridge leads straight to the mounds that cover the ruins of the palace of Sennacherib and the traditional tomb of Jonah.

(30) Not far from the ruins of ancient Nineveh, the country to the east becomes gradually mountainous. These mountain ranges separate the plains of Mesopotamia from the plateaux of

Persia. It was here that the Russians took
possession of all the mountain passes when co-
operating with the British troops in Lower
Mesopotamia.

Sheikh Matti is a Syrian Christian
monastery situated on the precipitous sides of
the Jebel Maklub, and overlooks the road that
leads from Rowanduz to Mosul. (*31*) There are no
carriage roads of any sort in this district, and
guns of every kind must be carried in sections
on the backs of camels or mules. It was
remarkable, therefore, how this difficult mountainous country was so successfully negotiated
by the Russian troops.

(*m*) **Carchemish.** Pharaoh Necho advanced in B.C. 609 with
Josiah his ally to take Carchemish, the capital of the Hittites. (See
Isaiah x. 9 ; Jeremiah xlvi. 2 ; 2 Chron. xxxv. 20). From cuneiform
inscriptions it appears that Carchemish was from about 1100 to 850 B.C.
the chief city of the Hittites who were masters of Syria from Biredjik
to Damascus.

(*n*) **Galatia.** The British civilian prisoners and the troops taken
by the Turks at Kut 'l Amara were interned at Konia and Nigdi.
These are places situated in the Galatia of the Bible familiar to Bible
students under the names of Iconium and Derbe. They were visited
by St. Paul on his first missionary journey (Acts xiii. 51, and
Acts xiv. 6). They were once inhabited by Galatians, to whom St. Paul
addressed his Epistle, and have more recently been occupied by Turks
and Armenians.

(*o*) **Nineveh** is especially famous for its association with the story
of Jonah, who predicted its overthrow. It was the capital of Assyria, a
country that adjoined Armenia in the north of Mesopotamia. When
Sennacherib, king of Assyria, was assassinated by his two sons, they fled
from Nineveh into the mountains of Armenia (2 Kings xix. 37).

VII.

Armenians Rescued near Antioch.

We will return once more to the Syrian coast in order to recall some other interesting events which took place in the Eastern Mediterranean, and resulted in the establishment at Port Said of a large camp of over 4,000 Armenian Refugees.

(32) A little south of Alexandretta, not far from the ancient city of Antioch, the Armenian inhabitants of six mountain villages decided to resist by force the attempt of the Turkish governor to drive them into banishment, as they had heard of the awful massacres that were taking place, and they refused to trust themselves to the Turks. They took up a strongly entrenched position on the heights of Mousa Dagh. All their flocks of sheep and goats were driven up the mountain-side. They secured 120 modern rifles and three times that number of old flint locks and pistols. They dug trenches, rolled rocks together, made strong barricades, behind which they planted groups of sharp-shooters.

In due course the Turks attacked them, but
were driven back, having suffered several
casualties. Two field guns were then dragged
up the mountain-side, and these began to make
havoc of the Armenian camp, but a young lion-
hearted sharp-shooter crept through the brush-
wood, made himself an ambush, and watching
his opportunity, disposed of four out of the five
gunners, which compelled the Turks to with-
draw their field guns. They then called the
people to arms from all the Moslem villages in
the district and gathered some thousands of
regular troops to attack the entrenched moun-
taineers. By sundown they had driven three
companies to within 400 yards of the Armenian
huts. A deep ravine, however, lay between the
Turks and the Armenians, which compelled
them to bivouac instead of pushing on that
night in the darkness. The Armenian leader
adopted a venturesome plan ; the Armenians
crept round the Turkish position in the dead of
night, then closed in suddenly at a given
signal with a fusilade. They had the advantage
of their foes, for they knew every crag and
thicket, so, with desperate courage they attacked
the Turkish forces, and threw them into be-
wilderment and alarm. The Turks were
obliged to retreat, losing more than 200 killed,

Armenian refugee camp at Port Said. (*page 27*).

French cruiser that saved 4,000 Armenians near Antioch.
(*page 29*).

Armenian children refugees at Port Said. (*page 29*)

and leaving behind much booty for the Armenians. Larger forces were then gathered together
by the Turks, but meanwhile their women-folk
had made two immense flags—on one of which
the words appeared in English, " Christians in
distress ; rescue." The other was a large white
flag with a red cross in the centre. These two
flags were fastened to tall trees, and watchmen
were set to scan the horizon from dawn to dusk.
The Turks continued to hurl their attacks
against the Armenians without gaining any
advantage, until one Sunday morning, the 36th
day of the Armenian defence, the watchman
was heard to shout, (33) " A battleship is coming,
and has answered our signals."

This was a French cruiser. Some of the
sturdy Armenians rushed down to the shore and
swam out to the boat that was lowered to
receive them. They narrated their story to the
Admiral of the fleet, and very soon four other
French boats and one English warship arrived
on the scene, whereupon the whole of the brave
Armenians were rescued and taken to Port Said.

(34) A camp was formed there, and these
refugees have been tenderly cared for by many
kind friends, and by the humane generosity of
the Egyptian Government.

The camp is well organised and the hundreds of sturdy children are being taught, not only to read and write, but many useful trades that will enable them to earn a living when the war is over. (35) They are to be seen at meal-times carrying baskets with the daily food supply for every tent.

VIII.

Side Shows and Lonely Outposts.

Another incident which took place not far from Alexandretta was the occupation by the French of the Island of Ruad, near Latakia. This island has proved to be very useful to the Allies in the maintenance of the blockade. Aeroplanes often appeared over Beyrout and the Lebanon, as well as over Jaffa and Gaza (*p*), where the Turkish encampments were constantly bombarded and their military positions frequently destroyed.

(36) Soon after the outbreak of war with Turkey, the German Consul at Haifa (*q*) led a party of Turks to desecrate the tomb of Napoleon's soldiers who were buried on the slopes of Mount Carmel. Herr Lange, another German, who had acted as Belgian Consul at Haifa, made the infamous proposal to the Turks that the English and French women left in Syria should be distributed amongst the Arabs.

(37) A French warship subsequently appeared at Haifa and administered a salutary lesson to

these inhuman vandals by destroying the German Consulate with shell fire. The Germans and the Turks have since been more circumspect in places that come within range of the guns of the Allied Navies.

(38) Cyprus (*r*) is situated in the East Mediterranean with its finger pointing to the port of Alexandretta. It was annexed to Great Britain when Turkey joined in the war, and was subsequently offered to Greece on condition that she came to the rescue of the Serbians. She refused, however, so the offer was withdrawn. Cyprus has constantly been utilised as a health resort for convalescent wounded British soldiers.

(39) The hill station of Troodos proved very useful for this purpose, and the large camp established there became very popular with the wounded soldiers who escaped thither from the great heat of Alexandria and Cairo.

(40) Salonica (*s*) was occupied by Allied forces soon after the evacuation of Gallipoli. This is one of the places where Germany hoped to secure a port at the Eastern end of the Mediterranean. It passed out of Turkish hands during the first Balkan War, and became a bone of

contention between the Greeks and the Bulgarians. It is a much coveted position, and became strongly held by Allied forces, as a base of operations for the liberation of Serbia.

(*41*) We will now leave the Mediterranean and proceed by Mount Sinai through the Red Sea to the Persian Gulf. On our way we should notice that British warships have more than once gone round the peninsula of Sinai for landing raiding parties, who attacked the Turkish positions as far as 60 miles inland ; they also destroyed the Turkish fortifications at the head of the Gulf of Akaba (*t*), whence an important caravan road leads to the interesting town of Kerak. (*42*)

It was reported that many Armenians, who were driven out from their homes in Armenia, were deported to this distant fanatical Moslem town. It is close to the important pilgrim railway from Damascus to Mecca, which is apparently being destroyed by the Arabs, who, under the Shereef of Mecca, have revolted against the Turks. On route to the Persian Gulf we should remember also the important British possession of (*43*) Aden, (*u*) where most trying military operations took place during the

early days of the war. Some Arab tribes were
stirred up by the Turks to believe that the
Holy War was making havoc of the British
Empire, and that there would be much booty
obtainable as a reward for their co-operation.
The British outposts were compelled to with-
draw to their more central positions as a result
of the Turkish onslaughts, which were, however, successfully repulsed, and the difficulties
of the situation that at one time threatened us
with serious trouble were in due course satis-
factorily overcome.

A touching little poem taken from *The
Times* sums up the situation at Aden and calls
forth our gratitude to the heroic defenders of
this lonely British possession.

HOME THOUGHTS.

The hot, red rocks of Aden
    Stand from their burnished sea;
The bitter sands of Aden
    Lie shimmering in their lee.

We have no joy of battle,
    No honour here is won;
Our little fights are nameless,
    With Turk and sand and sun.

East and west the greater wars
Swirl wildly up and down;
Forgotten here, and sadly
We hold the port and town.

The great round trees of England
Swell nobly from the grass,
The dark green fields of England,
Through which the red cows pass.

The wild-flowered lanes of England,
Hurt us with vain desire;
The little wayside cottage,
The clanging blacksmith's fire.

The salt dry sands of Aden,
The bitter sun-cursed shore;
Forget us not in England,
We cannot serve you more.

ADEN, 1916.

(*p*) **Gaza** is one of the oldest cities in the world, situated on the southern frontier of Palestine, mentioned in Gen. x. 19 as the "border of the Canaanites." After the conquest of the Promised Land by Joshua, Gaza was one of the three cities in which the Anakim still dwelt (Jos. xi. 22). The city was taken by Judah after Joshua's death (Judges i. 18), but in the days of Samson it is once again referred to as a city of the Philistines (Judges xvi.), where Samson displayed his marvellous strength in carrying away the city gates and in destroying the temple of Dagon. Philip the Evangelist was on his way from Jerusalem to Gaza when he overtook the Eunuch of Ethiopia, who had been to Jerusalem to worship (Acts viii. 26).

(*q*) **Haifa.** At the foot of Mount Carmel in the bay of Acre lies the modern city of Haifa, a port of growing importance, containing a large German colony and the Mediterranean terminus of the Turkish railways for Damascus and Mecca. In King David's time this was the home of Nabal, husband of the wise and beautiful Abigail, whose great possessions were in Carmel (1 Sam. xxv. 2). The spot is especially famous for its connection with the prophets Elijah and Elisha. It was on the slopes of Carmel that Elijah slew the prophets of Baal (1 Kings xviii. 19). Here was the home of Elisha (2 Kings iv. 25), and thence he proceeded to restore to life the son of the Shunammite woman.

(*r*) **Cyprus.** St. Barnabas, the companion of St. Paul, was a native of Cyprus which is only a few hours' sail from Cilicia, the home of St. Paul, where the friendship of the apostles may have begun in the schools of Tarsus. The two apostles visited Cyprus on St. Paul's first missionary journey. It was here that the Jewish sorcerer Barjesus was struck blind, where the Roman Proconsul, Sergius Paulus, became a believer, and where the apostle changed his name from Saul to Paul (Acts xiii. 8-12).

(*s*) **Salonica.** This is the famous Thessalonica where Paul and Silas established the first Christian Church, and whence they were expelled by the envy of the Jews (Acts xvii. 1-9). It was called Thessalonica after the sister of Alexander the Great, and in Apostolic time it was a port for the Via Egnatia and other important Roman roads.

(*t*) **Akaba**, which is situated at the head of the Gulf to the North of the Red Sea, is the port where " King Solomon made a navy of ships, in Ezion-geber, which was beside Eloth " (1 Kings ix. 26).

(*u*) **Aden.** It is recorded in 1 Kings x. 15, that King Solomon obtained gold from the kings of Arabia. The country between Aden and Sanaa is the only place in Arabia where gold is known to exist. Probably in this district also there were the forests which are mentioned in Isaiah xxi. 13.

IX

British and Russians Co-operate in Mesopotamia.

(*44*) Mesopotamia is reached through the great river, the Shat 'l Arab, with its picturesque banks, at the extreme end of the Persian Gulf. The British expedition to Mesopotamia was undertaken for three reasons:—Firstly, to check Germany's plans to extend the Baghdad Railway down to the Persian Gulf; secondly, to correct the impression spread among the Mohammedans by the Germans and Turks, that the British Empire was being ravaged by a revolution in India and Egypt, and the successful spread of the Holy War; and thirdly, to protect the important pipe line of 150 miles which leads from the oil wells to the refining factory at Abadan, (*45*) where over 6,000 men are employed. This oil refining factory is a most important asset to the British Navy. In June, 1914, Mr. Lloyd George in the House of Commons asked for £2,200,000 in order to secure our interests in the Anglo-Persian Oil

Company. He explained that the most modern
ships of the British Navy will be run by oil
fuel, that it was necessary for us to secure a
permanent supply, that all the oil-fields in
the world have practically been taken up by
American and other trusts, that the great oil
field of Persia and Lower Mesopotamia was the
only one still available, and that for 16 years
we have been watching the development of
those oil fields. Very soon after the outbreak
of war, the Turks made a raid upon the pipe
line and did some amount of damage until the
British troops cleared the country of hostile
forces, and within a few months the pipe line
was repaired. These military operations took
place near (46) Ahwaz and Shuster (v),important
centres of British trade on the Karun River,
whence proceeds an important caravan road into
Persia, made by a British firm for the conveyance of merchandise to Ispahan in the south,
and through Hamadan to Teheran in the north.
The same British firm that constructed this
road also maintains a weekly steamboat service
between Ahwaz and Busrah.

(47) The story of the occupation of Busrah is
well-known. It is an interesting place of great
commercial importance, and has often been

General Barrett and Staff arriving at Busrah. (*page 38*)

British steamboat preparing to leave Busrah for Baghdad. (*page 39*).

A creek in Busrah. (*page 39*).

called "The Venice of the East" on account
of the number of creeks which lead from the
Shat 'l Arab to the native town some two miles
away.

(48) The regular weekly service of British
steamers between Busrah and Baghdad was at
once suspended with the outbreak of war, and
one of the steamers which was at Baghdad
naturally fell into the hands of the Turks.
Another was at Busrah preparing to leave for
its 500 miles journey up the river, and it
managed to escape. Only flat bottomed steamers
can navigate the shallow waters and changing
sandbanks of the tortuous Tigris, so instead of
deep holds for the storage of cargo, these broad
paddle steamers carried the merchandise in a
barge which was lashed to the side of each ship,
and the passengers were accommodated by
hundreds on its spacious decks.

(49) When military operations began to develop
north of Busrah, it was found necessary to build
large numbers of native boats for conveying
troops across the extensive marshes that every-
where prevail in Lower Mesopotamia. Large
ocean steamers can proceed about 50 miles
north of Busrah to a place called Kurnah,

where some of the waters of the Euphrates
and the main stream of the Tigris together
flow into the great Shat 'l Arab. This
is the traditional site of the (50) Garden of Eden,
and the tree which has often been pointed out
as the "Tree of Knowledge of Good and
Evil" was planted by the Captain of one of
these British steamers about 30 years ago. It
was a desolate place under Ottoman misrule,
distinguished only for mud huts and a large
Turkish flag staff that stood by the side of the
Custom House, where the officer resided, whose
only concern was to collect the tax that was
levied upon every fruit-growing date palm.

(51) A little further up the river Tigris we
come to the Tomb of Ezra, which is a place of
pilgrimage resorted to by large numbers of the
Jews who dwell in Baghdad and Busrah.
There are more than 80,000 Arabic speaking
Jews living in the towns of Mesopotamia.

(52) The next town of importance on the Tigris
is the well-known town of Amara, which was
occupied by British troops after very arduous
military operations on both sides of the Tigris.
It was one of the centres for the extensive commerce in liquorice root.   British merchants

Amara on the Tigris, 100 miles from Busrah.   (*page 40*).

Inhabitants of Kut 'l Amara watching the arrival of a British steamer.
(*page 41*):

General view of Baghdad.   (*page 50*).

brought succour to large numbers of the starving inhabitants of these flood-afflicted plains by teaching them to dig up the liquorice roots and to pile them in heaps near their settlements, when, in due course, the merchants came along and purchased from the chiefs the many tons of liquorice root that were annually exported to England and America.

(53) It was quite a common thing to see a pile of liquorice behind the camel-hair tents of the dwellers in Mesopotamia.

(54) Our greatest conflicts in Mesopotamia have raged around the now famous Kût'l Amara. It was never a very important place, and the only excitement indulged in by the inhabitants was when the British steamers arrived on their weekly journeys between Busrah and Baghdad.

While General Townshend was invested in Kût 'l Amara he attempted to grow a certain quantity of vegetables for the supply of his troops. (55) The soil of Mesopotamia is particularly fertile, and as the aeroplanes supplied General Townshend with seeds, it was only necessary for him to keep his gardens well watered. This he was able to do by means of an interesting native "cherad," which brought up the water of

the Tigris in a very primitive way by means of
a large leathern bucket, which emptied the
water into a channel, through which it flowed
to the gardens beyond.

(56) The nearest point to Baghdad reached by
General Townshend is known as the battle field
of CTesiphon, which is marked by the ruins of
a wonderful arch that spanned the reception
hall of a palace built by Chosroes II. He was
the greatest monarch of the Persian Sassanian
dynasty, when Mesopotamia was a veritable
Garden of Eden and CTesiphon was its capital.

(57) It will be remembered that a very severe
battle was fought near these ruins, when
General Townshend succeeded in defeating the
Turks, and appeared to be making headway
towards the city of Baghdad. It was then that
enormous reinforcements were sent down to
stop his progress, and he was obliged to retire
from the fields of CTesiphon to his entrench-
ments at Kût 'l Amara.

(58) In order to relieve the pressure on Kût,
the Russians hurried forward their cavalry from
the Caucasus and captured Hamadan. This is
an important town situated between Baghdad
and Teheran at a distance of about 200 miles

Primitive irrigation " cherad " at Kut. (*page 41*):

Front View of arch at CTesiphon. (*page 42*).

Kasr-i-Shirin near the Turko-Persian frontier. (*page 43*).

from each place. The inhabitants number
about 25,000, many of whom are Jews who are
occupied in this busy industrial centre with gold,
silver and copper work. It possesses a shrine
where the tombs of Esther and Mordecai are
held in great veneration, and it occupies one of
the most beautiful sites in Persia, situated at a
great height in the mountains, and surrounded
by fine vineyards and orchards. It was here
that Alexander the Great offered sacrifices on
his return from India, and near the town are
two rock-hewn tablets with inscriptions that
bear the names of the kings Darius and
Xerxes. Hamadan was captured by the
Russians on December 16th, 1915, from the
Persian rebels who were led by the German
Commander, Prince Reuss.

(59) The Russian troops continued their
advance towards Baghdad, driving the Persian
rebels and some Turkish troops out of Kermanshah, and then subsequently capturing the difficult mountain pass of Kerrind, (60) which enabled
some of their forces to penetrate to the Persian
frontier city of Kasr-i-Shirin, (61) while a band of
Russian cavalry made a brilliant dash across the
mountains to the south, and joined the British
forces near Kût 'l Amara.

The surrender of General Townshend closed the first chapter of our struggles and triumphs connected with the war in the Bible Lands, but not the least of these triumphs was achieved by the brave troops who did their duty so well in the defence of Kût 'l Amara,

(v) **Ahwaz** and **Shuster**, on the Karun river, are not far from the ruins that mark the site of Susa, or Shushan, once the capital of Persia under Ahasuerus, where were enacted the incidents connected with Mordecai and Esther, as recorded in the book of Esther, as well as some of the incidents recorded in the book of Nehemiah (Esther i. 2 and Nehemiah i. 1).

(w) **Hamadan** is the ancient Ecbatana. Here are the reputed tombs of Queen Esther and Mordecai. The resident Jews erroneously regard Hamadan as the residence of Ahasuerus (Xerxes) which, however, in Scripture is declared to be at Susa (Esther i. 2, and ii. 3). It may be that this mistaken supposition has led them to locate in Hamadan the tombs of Esther and Mordecai. Hamadan is referred to in 2 Maccabees xi. ; in Judith i. 1 ; in Tob v. 9 ; and possibly in Ezra vi. 2.

X.

The Triumphant Sacrifice at Kut 'l Amara.

(62) It is too readily assumed that General Townshend's rapid advance on Baghdad was a military blunder, which resulted in an unnecessary sacrifice of 15,000 men. To those of us who know something of Mesopotamia and the situation which faced our authorities in the Eastern theatre of war, the dash towards Baghdad appears to have been the most triumphant piece of strategy which we were privileged to witness since the outbreak of war. It is of course necessary that British strategy should not be obvious to everybody, for it would then be obvious to our enemies and would fail to be strategy at all. The results alone assist us to arrive at the reasons for some of these so-called "side shows"; and the achievements of the force under General Townshend were undoubtedly worth even ιthe regrettable sacrifice of 15,000 heroic men. The facts are these :—

(63) First—elaborate preparations had been made by the Turks and Germans for a tremendous assault upon Egypt and the Suez Canal.

Many thousands of Germans passed through
Aleppo for Damascus, Jerusalem, and Beersheba.
The new railway line, completed since the outbreak of war through Beersheba and across the
Egyptian frontier, enabled German officers to
come from Berlin to the Egyptian frontier in
six days. Thousands of water pipes stored
up by the Germans in Alexandretta were
brought down to the south of Palestine and
laid for miles across the desert wastes that lead
to Egypt, whilst we were at that time badly
provided with the light railways and water pipes
necessary for pushing forward the large number
of troops needed to guard the Canal against a
well organised and well equipped expedition.
So this vital artery of the British Empire was
still a vulnerable point. The early months of
the year were considered most favourable for a
large army to cross the arid desert which
separates Palestine from Egypt. The Turks
were ceaselessly clamouring for the initiation of
this second Egyptian campaign. It was the
one expedition in which they were particularly
interested, as Egypt was to be Turkey's reward
for its aid to Germany. The Turks were
restlessly awaiting the assistance of the
Germans, for Serbia had been ravaged,
Bulgaria had been rewarded, but Turkey

had not yet received its coveted prize. So the Germans were about to yield to the Turkish demands, and therefore submarine activity began in the Eastern Mediterranean, the Senussi were aroused to attack Egypt on the west, Darfur in the south was developing its revolt. Dutch boats and Japanese ships were advised to avoid the Suez Canal, and to make their voyages round the Cape. The menace to the Canal, therefore, was a very real one ; and although we had troops enough in Egypt to deal with an invading army, yet in all probability our enemies could have succeeded in damaging the Canal and in blocking for many months our most important line of communications.

Secondly—the situation that was developing in Persia was just as serious. In December, 1915, the German Prince Reuss had managed to secure the allegiance of nearly all the armed forces of Persia, and the German-Persian corps under his command began to assume considerable proportions. Three thousand men of the Persian gendarmerie, under Swedish and German officers, had revolted, and were established in Hamadan, where they fortified the mountain passes that adjoined the Turkish frontier. In the same places there were also 6,000 religious leaders called *Mudjtahids*, (64) who were all armed and prepared to fight desperately in the cause of the Holy War. The headquarters of Prince Reuss were at Kûm, not far from Teheran, where he had several thousand irregular cavalry recruited from various nomadic tribes and placed under German officers. About 3,000 Turkish regular troops with two field guns had also managed to advance from Mesopotamia to Kermanshah. Prince Reuss was thus able to organise an army of at least 12,000 irregular cavalry, and an unknown quantity of marauders from certain nomadic tribes, who were well accustomed to robbery and loot. He quickly took possession of all the available cash and the securities which were found in the English banks at Ispahan, Shiraz and Yezd, and he was able to secure the services of a large number of Swedish gendarmerie officers by offering these adventurers much better pay than they had habitually received from the Shah. The Germans began to spread rumours of a Turko-German invasion of India by way of Baghdad and Persia. Their partisans stuck up posters urging that acts of violence should now be committed on Englishmen and Russians in accordance with the sanctions of the Holy War.

The British colony at Shiraz was taken captive
into the mountains, many *Persian notables* (65)
were arrested by the Germans to be kept as host-
ages, though the British and Russian consuls were
able to escape from Kirman to Bunder Abbas
in the Persian Gulf. The Kaiser had sent an
autograph letter to the Emir of Afghanistan
urging him as a faithful Moslem to respond to
the demands made upon him by the proclama-
tion of a Holy War. If this Persian situation
had really developed in accordance with
German expectations, the Turkish army would
have joined forces with Prince Reuss—would
probably have succeeded in arousing the
fanatical elements in Afghanistan, and would
have reached the Indian frontier with forces
that could not have been dealt with by half-a-
million men. Our authorities would have been
seriously to blame if they had failed to anticipate
the grave contingencies of such a formidable
menace to both India and Egypt. If General
Townshend and his troops had been kept in the
vicinity of Busrah until such times as a large
army could be prepared for an advance on
Baghdad, then undoubtedly the Germans would
have proceeded with the expedition to Egypt,
and considerable Turkish forces would have
been invading Persia before Sir Percy Sykes

had had time to organise his new and efficient gendarmerie, which was subsequently established at Kirman. It is evident that the Army Council saw an excellent opportunity for close co-operation with our Russian allies. Townshend was apparently ordered to advance with all speed and threaten Baghdad itself, while battalions of Russian Cavalry were hurried forward to deal with the irregular armies that were ravaging Persia.

(66) The fall of Baghdad would have been an serious blow to the Ottoman Turks. It would probably have influenced the inhabitants of Damascus, and perhaps have precipitated the Arab revolt in Arabia. In any case, it is now certain that General Townshend's advance on Baghdad compelled the Turks to give up their expedition against Egypt, and many thousands of troops with quantities of munitions were rapidly diverted and sent through Aleppo down to Mesopotamia.

Thirdly—There is still another interesting feature of the remarkable achievements of this little force that suffered so bravely in Kût 'l Amara. A few weeks after the battle of CTesiphon I was privileged to examine a broken kettle-drum which had been taken from

Group of Persian "Mudjtahids," or religious leaders. *page 48*).

Azeez Khan and Kurdish Troops. (*page 51*).

the Turks and had been sent to England by one of Townshend's officers. The inscription on this kettle-drum and the addresses on certain envelopes that were sent with it, confirmed my conviction that the *Kurdish Troops* (67) who ought to have been kept on guard against the Russian advance in the north, had likewise been hurried down to Baghdad to check the progress of our rash little army that was threatening the capital of Mesopotamia. It was not anticipated that the Russians would move forward in the depth of winter, and the Germans were mocking us in their newspapers by pointing out that the investment of our forces in Kût was a proof of the impossibility of the Allies being able to help each other, since the Russians could not come to save us. In point of fact, however, it turned out to be exactly the opposite to what the Germans supposed, for we were able, by successful co-operation, to help our Russian allies, and whilst our enemies were attracted to CTesiphon, the Russians, behind the backs of the Kurds, commenced to scale the snow-clad mountains of Armenia and sprang a surprise upon the depleted forces of the strongest stronghold of Asiatic Turkey.

(68) The capture of Erzeroum was a triumph

of the first magnitude, and has enabled the
Russians to continue their wonderful progress
to Trebizond, Erzinjan, Bitlis, and Moush.
Surely all this was worth the risk that was run
and the sacrifice that was made by the daring
advance of so small a force to the important city
of Baghdad. There is now no fear of an army
getting near enough to damage the Suez Canal,
but at a time when we were still unprepared, it was
General Townshend who saved the British
Empire from a serious menace to its most
vital line of communications. It was General
Townshend who checked an advance upon
India by detaining in Mesopotamia the
Turkish regular troops, whose presence in
Persia would have made all the difference to the
success of the German plans. They dared not
give up the siege of Kût 'l Amara, and while
they were there the Russian cavalry was able to
deal with the German led rebels until the menace
to India was entirely removed   It was General
Townshend and his 15,000 heroes who sped
the Russians into Erzeroum, who kept the
Turks from Persia and Egypt, and saved at a
critical moment the British Empire from a most
formidable menace.

GOD SAVE THE KING.

APPENDIX.

53

APPENDIX

V.—Turkey's Capital, Roadsteads and Ports.

VI.—From Alexandretta to Nineveh.

VII.—Armenians rescued near Antioch.

VIII.—Side Shows and Lonely Outposts.

APPENDIX

www.ingramcontent.com/pod-product-compliance
Lightning Source LLC
LaVergne TN
LVHW041203080426

835511LV00006B/723